Horatio B. (Horatio Balch) Hackett

Ceremonies at the Dedication of the Soldiers' Monument in

Newton, Mass

Horatio B. (Horatio Balch) Hackett

Ceremonies at the Dedication of the Soldiers' Monument in Newton, Mass

ISBN/EAN: 9783337134228

Printed in Europe, USA, Canada, Australia, Japan

Cover: Foto ©ninafisch / pixelio.de

More available books at **www.hansebooks.com**

AT

THE DEDICATION

OF THE

SOLDIERS' MONUMENT,

IN

NEWTON, MASS.

———— · ————

BOSTON:

S. CHISM, FRANKLIN PRINTING HOUSE,

No. 112 CONGRESS STREET.

1864.

THE MONUMENT.

FEELING that it is good to perpetuate the memory of those who give their lives to the service of their country, a distinguished citizen of Newton generously offered to give the sum of one thousand dollars, provided other friends would contribute an additional amount, sufficient to erect a Monument, which should stand as a permanent testimonial of the high appreciation of the inhabitants of Newton for their heroic dead.

The proposition was cordially welcomed by the people of the Town, and at a meeting held August 7th, 1863, Hon. J. WILEY EDMANDS, HENRY BIGELOW, M. D., Hon. WM. CLAFLIN, Hon. THOMAS RICE, Jr., Hon. D. H. MASON, WM. E. SHELDON, Esq., WILLARD MARCY, Esq., J. S. FARLOW, Esq., and JOHN C. CHAFFIN, Esq., were chosen a committee, with authority to erect a Monument.

In order that *all* might share in this grateful tribute, donations of one dollar were solicited from each inhabi-

tant, and nearly twelve hundred dollars were received from
this source. More than eleven hundred children of the
public schools contributed each a dime ; and the remainder
necessary to construct the Monument, to grade and sur-
round the lot with a suitable curb-stone, together with
the erection of an appropriate Entablature, has been
cheerfully given by the generous friends of the soldier.

The work has been completed at an expense of more
than five thousand dollars. The Monument stands upon
a lot of land given by the Town, in the Cemetery.
The Trustees of the latter corporation promise to keep the
lot in good order and condition.

The Monument is an octagonal shaft of Quincy
granite, resting upon a die and plinths of the same
material, and is twenty-eight feet in height. Upon the
front of the die are inscribed the words, " *In Memoriam
Perpetuam*." At a short distance from the Monument
an Entablature is erected, bearing the names of more
than forty soldiers who have died in the service, and the
inscription, " *Pro Patria Mortui Sunt*."

It was deemed accordant with the spirit of the enterprise, as well as suggestive of the duties and responsibili-
ties of the living, in this juncture of national affairs, to
celebrate the completion of the Monument with public
ceremonies, and dedicate it to the memory of the brave
heroes of Newton, who have fallen, or may fall, in this

struggle for liberty and good government. Accordingly, on the 23d day of July, 1864, this beacon memorial to the present and after times was solemnly inaugurated, in presence of a large and deeply interested audience, with the ceremonies described in the ensuing pages.

Hon. Thomas Rice, Jr., Chairman of the Board of Selectmen, presided on the occasion.

NAMES INSCRIBED ON THE TABLET.

LIEUT. EBEN WHITE,
ORLESTUS J. ADAMS,
JOHN ALLEN,
GEORGE BAKER,
GEORGE H. BAXTER,
WILLIAM R. BENSON,
THEODORE L. BRACKETT,
LEROY S. BRIDGMAN,
EBEN R. BUCK,
REUBEN L. BUTLER,
THOMAS W. CLIFFORD,
GILBERT A. CHENEY,
FERDINAND CHAMPION,
SETH COUSENS, JR.,
FREDERICK A. CUTTER,
WILLIAM FELL,
WILLIAM L. FREEMAN,
JOHN FORSYTH, JR.,
WILLIAM L. GILMAN,
LEOPOLD H. HAWKES,
PATRICK HAGGERTY,
THOMAS J. JACKSON,

ALBERT A. KENDALL,
JEFFERSON LARKIN,
CHARLES A. LEAVITT,
EDWARD LYMAN,
MICHAEL MARTIN,
DANIEL H. MILLER,
STEPHEN L. NICHOLS,
THOMAS C. NORCROSS,
WM. L. PARKER,
ALBERT F. POTTER,
JOSEPH R. PRATT,
WILLIAM H. RICE,
WILLIAM RAND, JR.,
JOHN B. ROGERS,
DANIEL SAWYER,
EDWARD H. TOMBS,
LUCIUS F. TROWBRIDGE,
MICHAEL VAUGHN,
CHARLES WARD,
GRAFTON H. WARD,
SAMUEL F. WOODWARD,

ADDRESS.

BY HON. THOMAS RICE, JR.

FELLOW CITIZENS:

WE have assembled in this quiet and beautiful cemetery, to dedicate this noble Monument, as a perpetual memorial of those brave sons and patriots of Newton, who, seeing our flag insulted, our homes threatened, our country in danger, buckled on their armor, and went forth in our defence and in the defence of their country, and fell martyrs in the midst of the struggle.

This Monument is built of the enduring and never-crumbling granite, that it may stand as long as the everlasting hills from whence it was taken ; that we may come beneath its shadow and teach our children and children's children to honor and revere the names of those inscribed upon its tablet.

Would to God that the last name had been inscribed — that the sacrifices which we have now made were sufficient to secure permanent peace ! But, my friends, such is not the case. We shall be called upon to add name after name to this honorable list, before this wicked and shameful rebellion is crushed, as it surely will be ; for it cannot be that this great nation, which has achieved its

own independence, and has so long been the asylum of
the oppressed of all other nations, is now to be destroyed
by its own internal dissensions. That the time may not
be far distant when this contest shall be over, should
be the ardent supplication of every Christian; that it may
end in the reëstablishment of the Union, the fervent
prayer of every patriot.

The promise made to our soldiers when they enlisted, —
" that should any of them be so unfortunate as to fall in
battle, their remains should be recovered if possible and
tenderly cared for," — has been faithfully carried out by
the Town, and most of those who have fallen now repose
in their native dust. But some still remain on southern
soil, where or how buried we know not. All we can
say of them is, they have fulfilled their mission, their
heroic deeds have passed into history, and their names
are engraven upon our memories.

This is a voluntary tribute of a grateful people to
perpetuate the memory and to hand down to future generations the names of those patriots who have fallen in
this second struggle for freedom and right. The people of
the Town have not waited until the war was over before
recognizing the services of those who have fallen in their
defence : but in the midst of the contest, while the government is calling for more men and more money, they have
gone forward in this noble work. We have done what the

Town and people may well be proud of. The Town has given and graded this beautiful spot, and the people have contributed the money to purchase this memento. It has all been done by voluntary subscription, and by all classes, from the princely merchant down to the humblest scholar in our common schools, that all might feel that they have a common interest in this patriotic work, and have done something towards perpetuating the memory of those who have proved good soldiers, and at the command of the Supreme Governor have laid down their arms and gone up higher.

Let us invoke the God of our fathers — that God of concord who presided over their deliberations when they laid the foundation of the Republic — to incline the hearts of our southern brethren to peace and submission to the legally constituted rulers of the nation; but failing this, let us pray that same God, who is also the God of battles, that he may grant victory upon victory to the Union arms, until every vestige of rebellion is swept from the land, and the flag of the United States — the symbol of her sovereignty — shall again wave, in undisputed supremacy, over a free, united, and prosperous people.

PRAYER.

BY REV. E. J. YOUNG.

O Thou, Father of spirits, in whom we live even when we die, as we stand upon this thy footstool we look to Thee and adore thy providence and supplicate thy blessing. Thou ordainest all events. Thou appointest the destiny of individuals and of nations. Thou art the God not of the dead but of the living, since all live unto Thee.

We bless Thee for our free institutions, which the sacrifices of our fathers secured and bequeathed to us. And we rejoice that the old fire which animated them is not extinct, but that Thou has given us new heroes and martyrs, who have not counted their lives dear, but have cheerfully given themselves for the country. They have brought to the altar a more precious gift than any of us, since they have laid down their lives for us. We remember with pride and thankfulness all that was heroic and excellent in their character, and all that was pure and bright in their example. And we come to-day to this hallowed spot with reverence and affection to commemorate their virtues, to celebrate their valor, to honor their memory, and to be quickened by their spirit. We come not to

weep for them, but to praise them; to express in prayer
and psalm, in eulogy and verse, our gratitude and admiration, and to dedicate to their perpetual remembrance
this free-will offering of all our people.

They need no monument to perpetuate their services.
Their memorial is in our hearts. Their names are im-
perishably inscribed in the nation's history. Their bodies
are buried in peace, and their names live forevermore.
They have consecrated this ground. They have made it
more illustrious than any pile we can place upon it. They
have added new glory to our town. And we desire to
show that we are not ungrateful. We desire to represent
by some enduring symbol our appreciation of their self-
sacrifice, and tell to future times the story of their fame.
We raise no broken shaft, emblem of an unfinished life,
but a solid column, pointing to the skies, nobler than any
arch of triumph, because reared in behalf of freedom and
of humanity. Here may their dust repose in peace, where
the heavens bend gently over them, where the flowers
bloom, and the birds sing, and the winds chant their
requiem. To all who shall come hither may this pillar
speak, declaring how glorious it is to die for our country,
and inspiring in all a resolute determination to be ever
faithful to liberty and to the laws. May it stand as a
sacred shrine, kindling in all hearts an ardent patriotism,
a deep sense of the sanctity of government, and of the

obligation of citizens to uphold and defend it. And
may victory soon change this into an obelisk of triumph,
and a redeemed and restored Union be our still grander
monument!

God of all grace and consolation, we remember with
sympathy the afflicted households, who have been called
to part with those that were dearest to them, who have given
their jewels — sons, brothers, husbands, fathers, — in this
sacred cause. May they rejoice that they had such to give.
May they be glad that they were willing to die. May
they feel that it is not in vain that they have fallen in
this great contest for civilization and popular government.
Thou hast ordained that everything which is most valuable
to man shall be bought with blood. Thou hast given thy
dear Son, who has offered himself for us all, and taught
us that we ought to lay down our lives for the brethren.
May these sorrowing ones believe, that it was not by chance
but by thy appointment that their friends were taken; that
they could not have died more gloriously; that they have
fallen in a conflict, not only for their own country and
age, but for the world and for all time. O may the words
of Him who assured his followers that in his Father's
house there were many mansions, and that it was expe-
dient for them that he should go away, comfort and sustain
their hearts. Let them not mourn that those they loved
have ceased to be mortal. Remembering that nothing

dies, and that these have only changed the mode of their existence, let them not seek the living among the dead, but follow their freed spirits to the world of larger liberty and life. And as they have sowed in tears, may they yet reap in joy. As they have gone forth weeping, bearing precious seed, so may they come again with rejoicing, bringing their sheaves with them.

Heavenly Father, as we dedicate this cenotaph to our brothers' memory, we would dedicate ourselves to the work which they have left unaccomplished. We feel that they have not gone from us, but that they are with us. And seeing that we are compassed about by so great a cloud of witnesses, we would pledge ourselves to Thee and to each other that their deaths shall not have been for nought. May their bravery rebuke our timidity, our selfishness, our despondency, and dissipate our doubts and fears. May their blood cry to us from the ground not to let the great purpose of our fathers fail. Amid the bewilderment and agitation of the time, give us eyes to see thy kingdom advancing to its completion, to the triumph of its principles and the establishment of its institutions. Go forth with us to the battle, and make us willing to accept and follow thy guidance. And may success enable us to plant a school and a church in every hamlet, and may the genius of Liberty walk with untrammelled feet, bringing blessings to every inhabitant, throughout the length and breadth of the land !

2

Bless our brave boys, whether on the land or on the sea. Bless those who are sick and wounded, more even in number than our great martyr host. Bless our rulers and leaders, and all our people. May we be knit together by suffering. and be ready to bear whatever Thou shalt lay upon us. Bless our town and all its interests, our homes. our schools, our seminaries, and our churches. May we be united in a common cause by common labors and sacrifices, and may we work together for the promotion of learning and charity, of good morals and religion. Bless those who are now to speak to us, and give them words of wisdom and inspiration. And wilt Thou arise and have mercy upon our Zion. Make us glad according to the days wherein Thou hast afflicted us. Establish Thou the work of our hands upon us, that all the causes of war may be removed, that every man may have the rights to which he is entitled as a man, and that our land may be indeed the land of the free, the refuge and the asylum for the oppressed of all nations. Forgive our manifold transgressions. Give repentance to those who are in arms against us. Make us worthy to live in this historic time. and keep us true to the ideas of the republic. Inspire us with faith, and hope, and fortitude, and courage. that we may not be dismayed by any temporary embarrassments. but may persevere manfully unto the end. And may this convulsion of the elements soon be followed by a clearer atmosphere and a purer sky, and our flag, no longer protecting the traffic in men as merchandize, be the herald of freedom, humanity, and justice, wherever it floats. We ask it as the disciples of Him who was slain, praying that Thy kingdom may come and Thy will be done on earth as it is in heaven. For Thine is the kingdom, and the power, and the glory, forever. Amen.

CHANT.

'T is holy ground —
This spot, where in their graves,
We place our Country's braves,
Who fell in Freedom's holy cause
Fighting for liberty and laws —
        Let tears abound.

Here let them rest,
And Summer's heat and Winter's cold,
Shall glow and freeze above this mould,
A thousand years shall pass away,
A Nation still shall mourn this clay,
        Which now is blest.

Here, where they lie,
Oft shall the widow's tear be shed,
Oft shall fond parents mourn their dead,
The orphan here shall kneel and weep,
And maidens grieve where lovers sleep —
        A broken tie.

Great God in heaven !
Shall all this sacred blood be shed,
Shall we thus mourn our glorious dead ?

O, shall the end be wrath and woe,
The knell of Freedom's overthrow,
　　　A country riven?

　　　It will not be!
We trust, O God! Thy Gracious Power
To aid us in our darkest hour.
This be our prayer — " O Father! save
A people's Freedom from the grave —
　　　All praise to thee!"

ADDRESS.

BY HORATIO B. HACKETT, D. D.

I HAVE supposed that I should be acting most in
harmony with the spirit of this service, if I connect the
remarks which I offer more especially with the memory
of those whom we are met here to commemorate, and the
reasons that we have for regarding the sacrifice of their
lives, costly as it is, as incurred for objects which justify
and ennoble the sacrifice. We have come here for
an earnest purpose. We desire, by an impressive act,
to declare our sense of the services and claims of the
men who have represented us in the camp and on the
battle-field, as defenders of our rights, as champions
of the nation's honor and safety, and who have sealed
their fidelity to this high trust, by giving up their lives
for us and our common country. Let it be remembered, too, that there are mourners among us here to-
day — fathers and mothers, brothers and sisters, widows
and orphans, — whose hearts bleed afresh at the sight of
the mournful emblems around us. If words may be
spoken that can alleviate their sorrow, and lead them
to reflect anew on the manner in which the sacrifices
they have been called to make are helping to accom-

plish the great ends of the national struggle, it becomes
us to utter such words, to suggest such thoughts.

As to my own part in these proceedings, I need not,
I hope, be anxious. You require nothing of me, on
this occasion, I am sure, beyond the performance of an
act of good will, — the offering with you and for you,
of a sincere, heartfelt tribute — that I can bring — to
the dear memory of the patriots, in honor of whom the
citizens of the town have set apart this sacred en-
closure and erected this monument, in this sleeping-
place of the dead.

The chairman has recounted to us the names of those
who have entered into the military service of the country from Newton, since the beginning of the war, and
have died in this service. They are more than forty in
number, and constitute our martyr-roll, as made up to
the present hour. Among these names you recognize
some which are among the names best known and
honored in the records of this ancient town. It may
confidently be said — the remark applies to our soldiers
living as well as dead — that, as a class, they represent
the public spirit, the enterprise, the intelligence, the
personal worth and social standing of our people, as
honorably to us as any equal number of men to whom
that office could have fallen. Among them are the
names of some, who, though not born among us, had

adopted our country as their country, and were willing
to perform the duties as well as enjoy the privileges of
American citizenship.

It will occur, also, to those of you who remember the
circumstances under which our soldiers have died, that
the manner of their death illustrates all the common
hazards and vicissitudes of war. Some perished by
casualty, in an unexpected way. Some contracted
disease, and after suffering for weeks or months, laid
down life's weary burden in tents and hospitals. Some
fell in the shock of battle itself, with victory almost
in their grasp; and others were brought back from the
field, death-stricken, to languish a while under the pain
of torturing wounds, and then pass away. It was the
privilege of some to have with them the presence of
friends to cheer their last hours, and to receive from
their lips messages of remembrance and love to those
in their New England homes whom they should see no
more; and others must die where they could receive
only a stranger's sympathy, and be laid in graves far
away from the homesteads in which life's young
morning opened on them.

But much as our departed friends may have differed
in such incidental ways, they were alike in this : — they
were all animated by the same generous, patriotic spirit ;
they all sprung forth at the call of their country, in the

hour of her distress ; they all earned that epitaph which you read on yonder tablet — " *Pro patria mortui sunt ;*" they all gave, each one, all that men can give — life itself — for their country ; and they all equally deserve, and shall equally receive, the gratitude of every American heart, and the wreath of immortal fame.

The monument which records their names, is to be the chief object of interest in this cemetery, in all future time. It shall not only, by its position, engage the first attention of those who enter here, but be remembered by them as they go hence, last and longest. No tombs will ever be built here, on which wealth or art can lavish such attractions as to draw aside the feet of men, to the neglect of this unadorned structure. Fathers will pause at the base of this column, and relate its history to their children. It will be told here who these patriots were ; what sufferings they underwent in their day and generation, to make this land an abode of peace, happiness, and liberty, to those who should live after them ; what principles they upheld in life and in death ; and what lessons should be drawn from their example by those who enjoy the fruits of their patriotism and self-denial. The mute instructor, which stands here before us, will pour such teachings on the ear of generations yet unborn. The benedictions of a grateful pos-

terity will rest on the memory of our heroes, and keep
it fresh forever.

> " How sleep the brave, who sink to rest,
> By all their country's wishes blest!
> When Spring with dewy fingers cold
> Returns to deck their hallowed mould,
> She there shall dress a sweeter sod
> Than Fancy's feet have ever trod.
>
> By fairy hands their knell is rung,
> By forms unseen their dirge is sung;
> There Honor comes, a pilgrim gray,
> To bless the turf that wraps their clay;
> And Freedom shall awhile repair
> To dwell a weeping hermit there."

Then farewell to them, henceforth, as to their living
presence among us; but hail to them as they ascend to
take their places among the unseen influences which
are to pervade our history, and mould the national
spirit in all time to come.

From these more strictly commemorative remarks, I
proceed to glance, in a hurried manner it must be, at
two or three considerations of a general character.

Here we are, on this mid-summer day, almost in the
middle of the fourth year of this terrible civil war,

which has deluged the land with blood, has brought
bereavement and sorrow into thousands and thousands
of happy homes, has thrown into disorder the nation's
finances, and hangs over us still as a cloud which has
not yet discharged upon us all its violence and fury.
Our flag may have risen high enough, it has risen high
enough to show which way its folds point; but we are
not at the end yet. Battles are still to be fought.
Hopes and fears are to agitate the public mind. Other
victims must be laid on the altar. The voice of sorrow
must be heard in dwellings which the destroyer has
passed by hitherto. Our burdens of taxation may be
increased an hundred fold. We would hope for things
less grievous; but perhaps before we reëstablish our
government throughout the entire land, it may be found
that we have as yet dipped our feet only into the brink
of the waters, which are to surge and dash around us,
till we see their lowest depths.

Contemplating such a possible future, and in view of
such a past as we have had already, the question is
forced upon us, to which I adverted at the beginning:
*Do the objects at stake in this war require and justify all
this cost?* In giving a brief answer to this question, I
prefer to mention moral reasons rather than political,
though I confess the line which separates them is a nar-
row one, and though I may lose the advantage of giving

the answer to the question which many might consider the most decisive.

I believe fully, earnestly believe, in the accountability of one age to another, of one generation of men to other and subsequent generations. Out of this principle springs an obligation resting on us, to pursue this war to its proper end, as strong as ever rested on any people, summoned to a great crisis in their affairs. It is a social law of the utmost significance, and one that has the highest of all sanctions, that men live not, men die not, unto themselves; their actions in one period stretch onward, and affect the condition of others, for good or evil, through all time. Our fathers, in the conflict of the Revolution, met that responsibility in their day; and, as a consequence, established for us this government, under which, until the hand of parricides was lifted up against it, we enjoyed a prosperity which had no parallel in the world, and was actually the world's envy; and yet the reasons for the war of the Revolution, in which they persevered twice as long as we have been struggling now, were utterly trifling compared with those which demand of us energy and self-denial to maintain this fabric of government and hand it down to those after us. Observe the nature of the trust committed by them to us. They put this government into our custody, to keep, not for one part of the country, but for every part; not for

New England alone, but the West also; and not for the East and West alone, but for the South as well as the North, and for the South just as much and as distinctly as for the North. As parties, therefore, to this compact, we who are living now have no more right to consent to the destruction of the government at the South than at the North; and the man, in this point of view, who is willing to see the flag of his country trodden in the dust on the soil of South Carolina, is just as false to his obligations as the man who would stand by and see it dishonored on the soil of Massachusetts.

Nor is this all. This compact, in its moral implications as well as political, meant, that the government should be permanent as well as universal. It was won at such cost and put in operation, not for the inhabitants of this land merely who should live between 1776 and 1861, but for all throughout this vast domain, who should ever come forward here to breathe the breath of life and be capable of enjoying the blessings of self-government and national security. Mark, then, the solemnity of our position. These blessings, in order to reach their destination, must flow through our hands. We stand in the exact and only line of transmission through which they can be carried along the track of time to the millions unborn, whose condition is to depend on what we do or fail to do. If, then, these blessings are stayed in

their course, at the precise moment when the responsibility for their preservation is laid on our shoulders, do
we not incur the reproaches of those who shall follow
us as well as of those who were before us? We do,
undeniably ; for, by the same unfaithful act, we frustrate
the work of our fathers, and we rob their descendants
of the heritage which was theirs.

Nor are we at liberty to forget the relations which
we sustain to other peoples. Providence has put it
into our power, if we are true to His orderings, to be-
come the benefactors of mankind on a scale of grandeur
unexampled heretofore ; not by any open crusade for
the rights of man, but by the silent operation of our
example, and the opening of a refuge here for the
oppressed, of every clime and color, who would
secure a better condition for themselves and their children.   Oh! how often in the fairest portions of Europe,
as I have seen the poverty and misery, the ignorance
and degradation of the masses of my fellow-men, ren-
dered not less but more painful by contrast with the
brilliant civilization, wealth, and luxury, of the favored
few — as I have turned my eye from these sights to the
happy spectacle here at home — how often and earnestly have I thanked God that he put it into the hearts of
our ancestors to come here and inaugurate a new type
of civil polity on these shores.

Recollect that the governments of the earth, be it as it may with the people, the governments which exist so extensively for the benefit of those who administer them, are not with us, but against us. This is a trite theme, I know; but do not the revelations of every hour bring it before us with new and startling vividness? Whence is it that the organs of public intelligence which speak for the monarchists of the old world, hold up to admiration the murders and piracies of a buccaneer, who burns and sinks peaceful ships of commerce, but skulks from sea to sea or runs into neutral ports to escape an armed foe; and, when at length the waters close over the guilty career of the pirate, lament it as an event which excites regret throughout kingdoms and empires, and treat it almost as an affront to be avenged? Ah, I see in that spirit evidence which no fact could express with greater energy, that my country's government is the people's government as distinguished from that of the rulers; and, while it would degrade none, would place all on a juster level in their political rights and means of personal happiness. It is no exaggeration to say, as is so often said, that the triumph of despotism would be complete throughout the earth, that the cause of republican liberty would be lost for all men, and every where, if it be lost here and by us.

On the issue of this war, too, hangs suspended the

destiny of three or four millions of human beings among
ourselves, and of the long line of their descendants,
through an indefinite future. A wonder-working Providence, as we may well call it, has made it dependent on
the success of our arms, whether they shall be free or
left in hopeless bondage; whether the promised boon
in their behalf shall prove a reality, or a delusion and
mockery of their hopes.

If, then, being men, we are not ashamed to own that
nothing human is or should be alien to us, that we *are*
bound to our race by ties which we cannot and would
not sever, do not such relations make it incumbent on
us to defend a government which has such bearings on
human welfare, at all hazards, against all assailants at
home and abroad?   And, if it be true, that

> "The fittest place for man to die
>   Is where he dies for man,"

then do not our sons and brothers, who fall in behalf of
such a cause, add to their title as patriots that, also, of
friends of their race?

If you would find reasons why this rebellion should
array against itself all the moral instincts of the human
soul, think, I pray you, — of a thousand things, I had
almost said, which, for brevity's sake, I can only indi-

cate. Think, for example, of the pitiful pretense that
the government was oppressive, though administered in
fact during almost the entire period of its existence by
the very class of men who are now in arms against it ;
think of the perjury of such leaders among them as
Davis and Breckenridge, who as senators could stand
up before the nation, and, with an appeal to the heart-
searching God, swear that they would maintain the
union of these States inviolate, though in secret they
had already pledged those same perjured right hands to
each other for the overthrow of the Union ; and, of that
conduct, not unlike this, of the commander of their
armies who betrayed no consciousness of self-degradation
in being willing to loiter at Washington, week after week,
and month after month, in order, before his own open
defection, to find out the military secrets of the government, for the benefit of his accomplices, though as much
a traitor then as we know him to be now, when we
see his blood-stained sword flashing before our eyes ;
think of the clandestine transfer to their territory, of
guns and munitions of war from our forts and arsenals,
to which their agents put into office by our votes had
the key ; think of the attempt to slay the President
elect, on his way to the capital, by a band of hired
assassins ; think of the massacre of men and women
on the mountains of East Tennessee, because they

3

wished to live and die under the flag of their country;
think of the butchery of disarmed, helpless prisoners,
for no other crime than that of preferring to be free
rather than slaves; and, above all, think of the object
of all this aggravated treason, avowed and boasted of
by its abettors — the establishing of a great slave
empire, which being established must inevitably give
law to the American continent. Do not such men
deserve the terrible name, which it makes the soul
shudder to think of — enemies of mankind! Was
there ever a great national movement, having for its
object a purpose so wicked, which subsidized so many
subordinate villanies for its accomplishment? And
was there ever any emergency in any people's history
which called like our own, upon all that is manly and
noble in human nature, to stand up and declare, with
vehement protest before the universe, the scheme
shall not be consummated?

If any would judge whether we have a cause that is
worth suffering for and dying for, let them think of the
condition in which we should be if we fail to crush this
rebellion and save the republic. There can be no compromise; it has been tried again and again, and to no
purpose. How can this word of delusion be any longer
on any man's lips? Does any one really think that the
rebels are fighting for a compromise? If any person

supposes that, he must have extraordinary ideas of the
nature of a compromise. Compromise! of what?
They had the same privileges under the common government that we had, and by their own confession more
than we had; and they were assured after they began
their work of anarchy that they should have them still,
if they would lay down their arms and spare the government. They spurned the offer, because they were
aiming, it is evident, at something beyond compromise,—
at something which nothing but the destruction of the
government could give them. The insurgents deserve,
at least, the credit of this sincerity:—they have put
their intentions before us, without equivocation or am-
biguity; and if any one among us is deceived it cannot
be because any artifice on their part has deceived him.

Every day, by words and by deeds, they thrust back
upon us this idea of compromise, with scornful defi-
ance. "No," they say, "we mean to bring you, by
force of arms, to our terms — surrender of your capital,
destruction of your nationality, boundaries that will give
to us all the slave-states, the conqueror's share of the
common territory and navy, indemnification for losses
and expenses, the comity of crossing your borders for
slave-hunting, and the right to adjust, at the point of
the bayonet, all questions that may grow out of that
delicate diplomacy;—we mean to fight till we bring

you to these terms, or till you, by force of arms, take
from us the power to enforce such terms." This is
explicit, and ought to be understood. Is it compromise?
Or the subversion of the national sovereignty and independence? The alternative plainly is that we must
conquer or be enslaved. Give to them, after being separated from us, if that were possible, a respite of twenty
years or less, for recuperation and preparation, and the
apathy on our part which would enable them to gain
that respite, would enable them if not by renewed and
successful war, yet by means of their political ascend-
ency and the influence of southernizing commercial
treaties which we should be led to form with them, to
put the heel of their power on our necks as their vassals
in effect, if not in name. I repeat it — we must conquer
or be enslaved. This war is a war for the freedom
of the white race as well as of the blacks.

Shall we complain of the taxes? It cannot be said
that they are severe as yet, compared with those to
which nations are accustomed to submit in time of war.
But look at the other side. Suppose two nations such
as the people of the North and South would form, were
existing here, side by side. Who is to pay for the im-
mense standing army, on which you would rely, though
with vain reliance, for the maintenance of peace between
two such nations? Who is to pay for the fortifications,

which would bristle in every port and on every head-
land, and stretch across the continent from the Pacific
to the Atlantic? At whose expense are those intermi-
nable border wars to be waged, which would be inevi-
table between powers separated by so many clashing
interests, and embittered toward each other by the
memory of the hostility of these days? If a single
Alabama can make such havoc of our commerce, what
must be the fate of that commerce if exposed to the
depredations of a whole fleet of such scourges of the
ocean? Is a civil war, which has continued only three
or four years, so oppressive? And what then must be
a perpetual civil war? Nay, if it be written in the
book of fate, I should say rather in that of our own
degeneracy, that we must succumb, then it is already
true as a virtually existing fact, that heavier mortgages
to the Southern Confederacy lie at this moment on the
ships which sail out of Boston harbor and on these
broad acres around us which men cultivate who call
themselves free, than would be required during centu-
ries for the liquidation of the present war debt, though
that were increased ten thousand times.

Our soldiers fight and fall, bleed and die, to save us
and our posterity from this state of things. It is a
costly sacrifice; but is it not for worthy ends? No
human eye, it is true, can penetrate all the future. But

of this we may be certain, that nothing half so fearful
can lie before us if we go forward in the path of duty
and patriotism, as awaits us inevitably if we go back or
stop here ; and nothing remains for us, therefore, if we
have any manhood in us, but, with God's blessing, to
" fight it out on this line" of duty and patriotism, as
long as there is a shot left in the locker.

There was a legend in the old Greek history, con-
nected with the battle of Marathon, which arose, perhaps, from a popular superstition, but which, like so
many of the imaginations of that ingenious people, was
fraught with truth, and might have been invented by
the wisest sages, with credit to their sagacity. It is
full of meaning and instructive for us. An amphithea-
tre of hills looks down on the plain where the Persian
horde was trampled in the dust by Grecian valor, and
the tide of Asiatic despotism and barbarism was rolled
back from the shores of Europe. The surges of the
sea on which the ships of the invaders rode so proudly,
may be heard, breaking at the foot of these hills, and at
a little distance from the shore, may be seen still the
hillock beneath which the bones of the Athenian con-
querors were buried. The Greeks, now, believed that
this great battle was continually reënacted on this memo-
rable spot. They believed that as they stood at night
on these hills, they could see through the mists the

forms of warriors moving across the plain, and could
hear the clash of armor, pæans of victory from their
countrymen, and cries of despair from the vanquished.
Of the value of this susceptibility of the Greek mind,
who can doubt? It was worth more, infinitely, to that
world-conquering race, than city walls, than bulwarks,
than navies. It was a power in their history ever
present, which kept alive the spirit of heroism, and
nerved them for other conflicts and victories.

Not unlike this, except more beneficent, more efficient,
shall be the remembrance of these days to our children
and children's children. Our battles, too, shall be
re-fought; the voices heard in them shall never cease
to speak to us. Mysterious as it may seem to our finite
comprehension, yet how often has it been shown to be
sublimely true —

> " God's most dreaded instrument
>   In working out a pure intent
>   Is man arrayed for mutual slaughter."

No nation can be truly great or exist long, without
a history which has in it soul and inspiration. Account
for it as you may, there can be no doubt that we had
nearly outlived *our* history. The old examples, perhaps
because we had drifted away so insensibly from the
principles which they sanctioned, were losing their in-

fluence over us more and more. The time had come
when some new shock, a fiercer discipline, was needed,
to bring out and strengthen the nation's character. It
is true of national blessings as of individual, that we must
learn to value them by knowing what it is to labor for
them and make sacrifices for them. A people whom
the great Ruler of nations would have live and not per-
ish, must be brought back to this experience as often as
they are in danger of forgetting the steps by which they
became great and prosperous. We are passing through
the trials which shall perform for us that salutary work.

Out of this war shall arise a juster estimate of the
transcendent privileges of our American form of government. We are indebted to it already for illustrations
of a true public spirit as noble, as elevating as the world
ever saw. We are gathering up from it every day the
materials of the richest heritage that one age can trans-
mit to another. Our lost history shall be restored to
us. Examples of genuine Christian patriotism and
heroism have appeared during this struggle, worthy
of perpetual record, — examples of fealty to principle
which holds everything — life itself — subordinate to
that supremacy, — deeds of suffering and valor never
surpassed, performed by men in the ranks, who may
be counted by thousands and tens of thousands, and performed by them intelligently, consciously in behalf of

what is right, against the violation of sacred compacts,
against injustice and oppression, against treachery to
future generations, whose interests we are appointed to
guard.   I cannot doubt, as I have confidence in the
wisdom of the Supreme one, that He means by these
fiery trials that we should be made a better, a stronger,
a happier people, and be fitted to act more worthily the
part as dispensers of blessings to the world, which His
Providence had seemed to mark out for us.

I have but one other brief thought to suggest, and
that may not improperly lead us to retrace our steps, and
come back once more to the tomb from which we took
our departure.   The example of the dead should in-
struct the living.   The manner of the service which we
owe to our country may be different, but the measure
of it is the same to all; and that has been illustrated in
the self-devotion of those whose memory we honor here
to-day.   It is well for us to build their monuments; but
we bestow the truest honor upon them, when we take
up the work which by reason of death has fallen from
their hands, and carry it forward, in their spirit, to its
consummation.   Happy, oh! thrice happy they, who,
having fallen for their country, rest now in their graves,
compared with those who survive a country lost through
their neglect and cowardice.

I am reminded of a sentiment of the true-hearted

patriot, on whom Providence has devolved the task of guiding our ship of State through this night of tempest and gloom, which should be engraven on all our hearts. It was well said by him, at Gettysburg, that the proper use of an occasion like this, as we bend over the graves of our martyr-soldiers, " is to dedicate ourselves anew to the living work of saving the country for which they died." We learn our duties most safely by inferring them from the providential circumstances under which life has been allotted to us. Let it then be brought home to the heart of every true man and woman in this land, that our appropriate work in this our day and generation is, by every patriotic duty performed, by self-denial practised, by life itself surrendered if need be, to thwart this rebellion, and save our imperilled country and its liberties, to the glory of God and the good of mankind.

HYMN.

SOFT winds are mournfully sweeping,
　　Whispering oak branches wave,
Where your loved ashes are sleeping,
　　Forms of the true and the brave!
Silence reigns breathless around you,
　　All your stern conflicts are o'er,
Deep is the sleep that hath bound you,
　　Trumpet shall rouse you no more.

Sweet and serene be your slumber!
　　Hearts for whose freedom ye bled.
Millions, whom no man can number,
　　Tears of sad gratitude shed.
Never shall morn, brightly breaking,
　　Enter your chambers of gloom,
Till the last trumpet awaking,
　　Sound through the depths of the tomb!

Earth's shadowy years soon will leave us,
　　Heaven's blissful morn then arise ;
Sorrow's night then will forsake us —
　　Farewell to all weeping eyes.
There will the Lord our Redeemer,
　　Unveil his bright, beaming face,
Shining in glory serener,
　　Fairer than earth's loveliest rays.

POEM.

BY REV. S. F. SMITH, D. D.

SOFTLY, their labors done. the patriots rest,
Honored in life. and in their memory blest ;
Living, they earned and won a glorious name ;
Dying, they found at once immortal fame.
Spring o'er their relies strews its fragrant flowers,
Smiles in the sunshine, weeps in dews and showers ;
And Summer spreads its freshest, sweetest bloom,
Green as their memory o'er their honored tomb.

And Nature wraps around them, where they rest,
The dear old flag, in dyes she loves the best ;
Blue, in the starry arch that bends above,
Like mothers, bowed to kiss the babes they love ;
White, — when the earth is mantled o'er with snow, —
A bridal honor for the brave below ;
And red, when round their couch sweet Autumn weaves
A burnished beauty with her fiery leaves.
The glorious banner wraps the rolling year,
And spreads its folds around the sleepers here,
As thousands weep the heroes who have bled,
For each a tear, a blessing on each head.

From granite crypts kind Nature fondly rears
The pillar, hewed by love and wet with tears;—
The fitting record of the men who stood
True to the right, 'mid fire and death and blood;
And history writes their names high on her scroll,
Heroes, of granite will, but loving soul.

Stand, massive record, as the heroes stood.
When swept the storm, when swelled the angry flood!
The names, engraven on the rock, are thine;
The men who bore them grateful hearts enshrine.
Dew-drop and rain and grateful tear may dry,
But noble deeds once done can never die.
Though marble shattered may betray its trust,
And pile and column crumble into dust,
Heroic deeds a deathless pile shall raise ;
A land redeemed preserves their lasting praise.

Not here alone their monument is reared,
To memory sacred and by love endeared;
Where'er the oppressed the bonds of sorrow wear, —
Where'er the slave lifts up his humble prayer,
Their high memorial lives, in fetters riven, —
A pile, whose base is earth, whose crown is heaven.
These were the men who firm in battle stood,
The men who shrunk not from the flame or flood;
Who gave to Freedom's cause their noblest powers.
Born for the nation's need, they died for ours.
Weep for their memory. Would they had not died!
Sing for their memory!—'t is the nation's pride.

They bore the toil, they earned the grand *eclât ;*
Proclaim their memory with the glad hurrah.

No hostile foot this sacred soil shall tread ;
No hostile banner wave above the dead ;
No warlike clarion break their sweet repose,
Calm as the dew-drop, resting on the rose.
But grateful tears their relics shall bedew,
The loved, the brave, the trusted, and the true.
Mothers and maidens, gathered round the tomb,
Shall sigh and sing the soldier's "welcome home."
Mourning the fallen, to their country given,
With sweet will yielding to the will of Heaven.
  " O grief unspeakable !" yet faith can see
Rifts in the cloud —"Our country, 't is for thee !"
And thus, resigned, with calm and holy trust,
Mother and maiden leave the hallowed dust ;
With woman's faithful heart their grief restrain, —
Willing to make such sacrifice again.

Breathe soft, O winds, around this treasured trust !
Keep, holy earth, this loved and honored dust !
Sing your sweet pæans, birds of varied wing !
In heaven's free air let warbled freedom ring.
Keep nightly watch, ye stars, above their bed,
Teaching the living, smiling o'er the dead !
Though hid by tempests, gently still ye shine,
Keeping in heaven's blue field your march divine ;
Though clouds may darken, though the tempest lowers,
Heaven keeps its stars unharmed, as we shall, ours.

Clouds cannot quench them; God's great word, once given,
Their light shall flash again, full in mid heaven;
And every star that keeps its shining way,
Glimmers, prophetic of the coming day.

Lift your tall crests, ye trees, in verdant pride!
A hundred storms your sturdy trunks have tried;
Tempests have beat in fury round your head,
But still ye cheer the living, shade the dead!
So when the raging blast has spent its power,
And clouds no more in angry blackness lower,
The nation, saved, shall bloom in peace anew,
Its genial shade the weary pilgrim woo;
Thousands repose beneath each sheltering bough,
Made stronger by the blasts that toss it now;
The anxious watcher mourn no kindred slain,
The soldier seek his home and babes again;
The sword be sheathed, and war's dread tumult cease,
And spotless banners wave in joy and peace.

HYMN.

BY REV. S. F. SMITH, D. D.

TAKE these choice treasures, gentle earth,
 And shield them in thy faithful breast,
Gathered like gems of priceless worth,
 And brought among thy dead to rest.

Take this new honor, reared in love,
 Where sleep the trusted and the brave,
Pointing the mourner's faith above,
 To Him who takes, to Him who gave.

Round this fair shaft let summer leave
 Its fragrant airs at morn and even,
And golden clouds in sunlight weave
 Pathways of glory into heaven.

Again the flag of peace shall float
 O'er all the land, from sea to sea;
O'er all the land shall swell the note
 Of Freedom's final Jubilee.

We build the shrine, we sing the brave,
 Yet own how vain are human boasts;
In God alone is power to save,
 Our trust is in the Lord of Hosts.